READING & WRITING

ROBERT PACE

book 1

© Copyright 1983 by LEE ROBERTS MUSIC PUBLICATIONS, Inc.   Katonah, N.Y.
International Copyright Secured   Printed in U.S.A.   All Rights Reserved

Stepping

As you are playing "Stepping", be sure to look at the page and *not* at your hands.
Do this several times until it is easy.

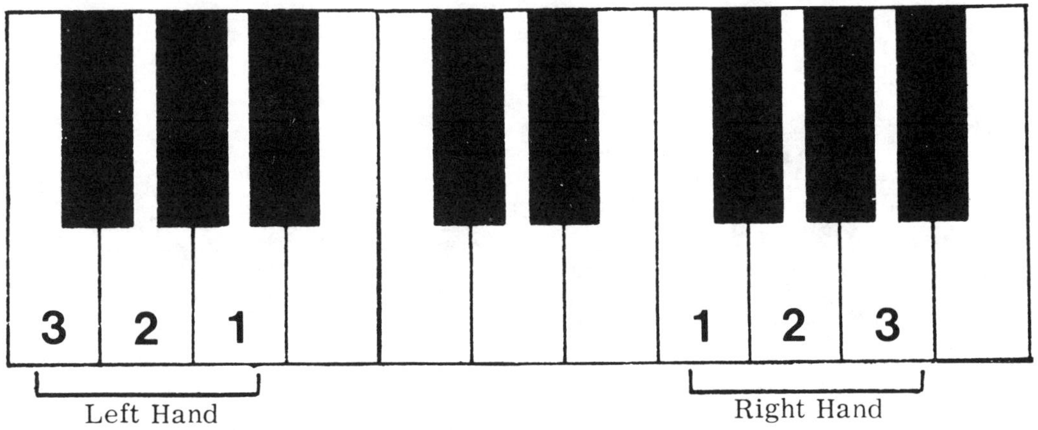

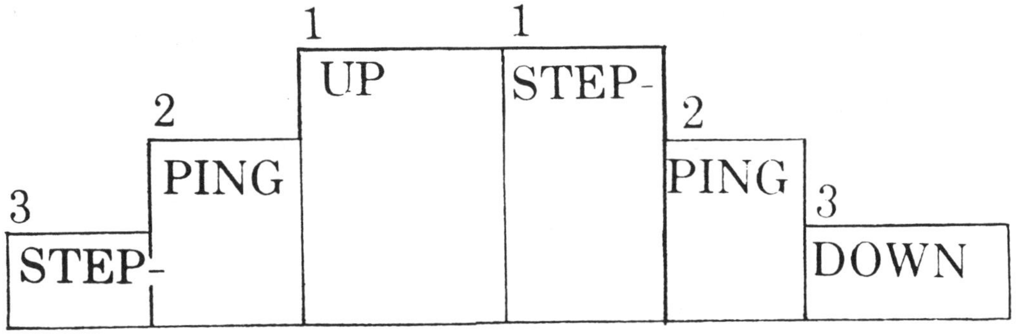

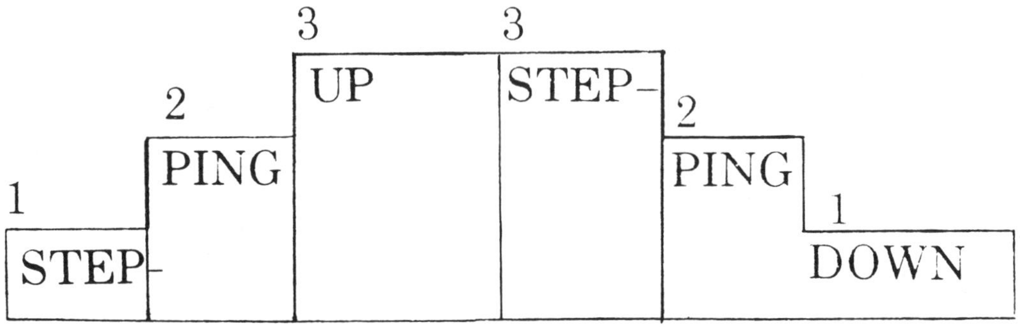

Find three white notes just below the twins as shown here and play "Stepping" again.

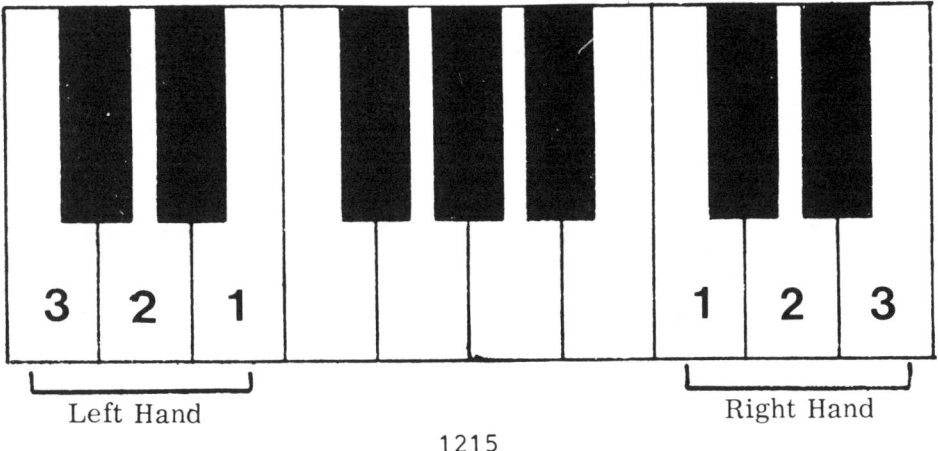

The Piano Keyboard

Darken each group of 3 black keys.
Then, as you keep your eyes on the page, *feel* the three black keys of your piano to find the "triplets" without looking down.
Try this until it is easy.

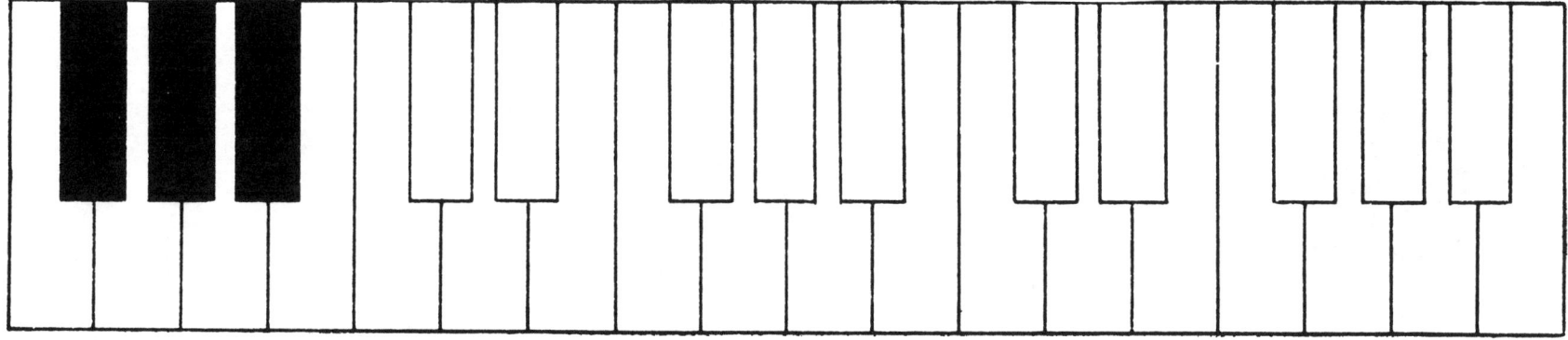

Now, darken the groups of 2 black keys.
Again, keep your eyes on the page as you find the twins on the piano keyboard without looking down.

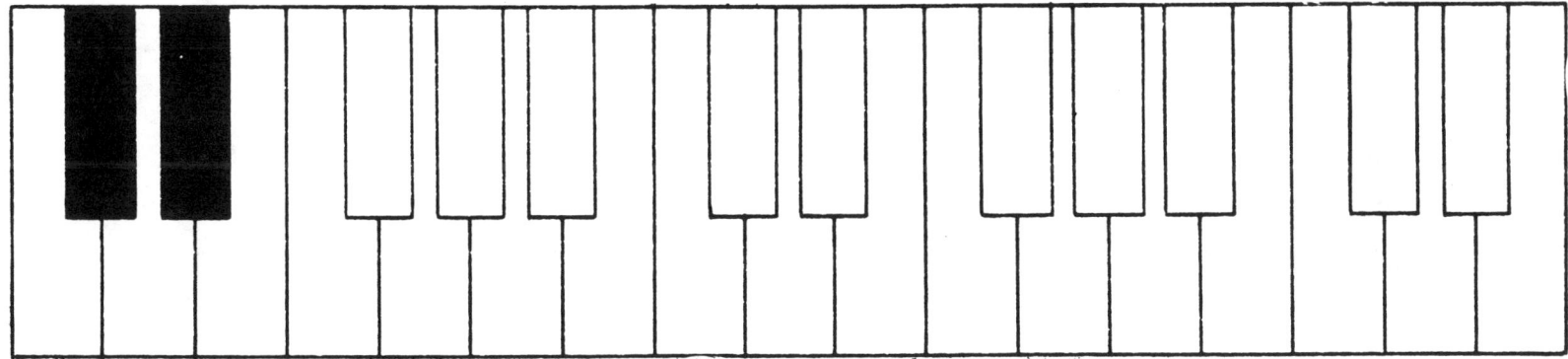

Finally, mix the two's and three's.
Be sure to find them without looking down.

Hot Cross Buns

1. Sing and shape the melody.
2. Sing and clap the rhythm.
3. Sing and play the melody in the air.
4. Sing and play the melody on the piano.

Right Hand

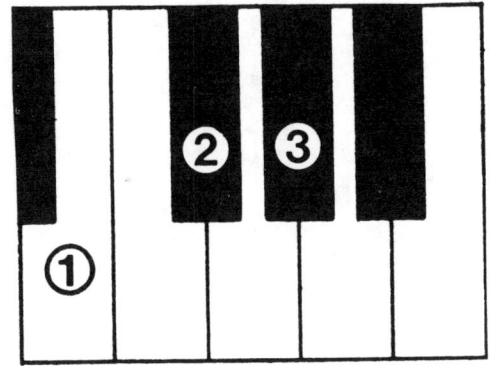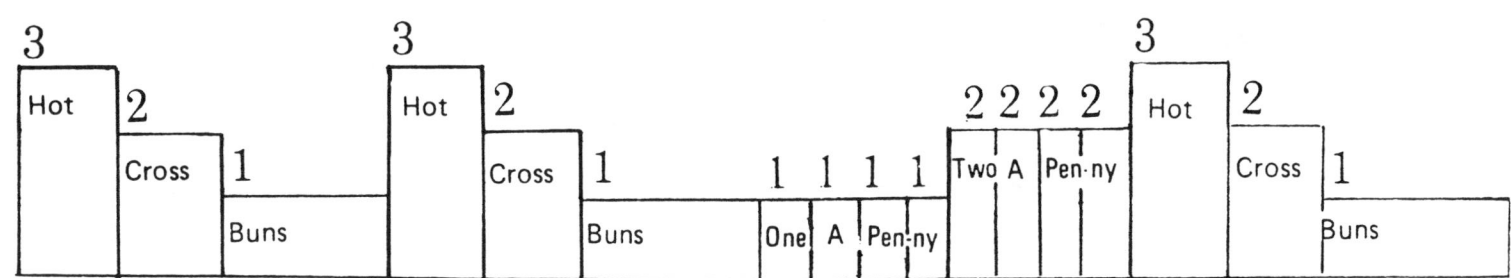

Left Hand

Now, play "Hot Cross Buns" in the left hand.

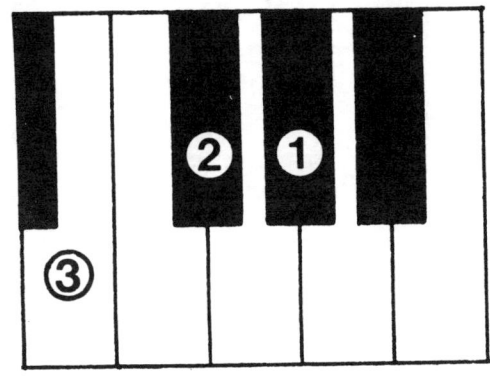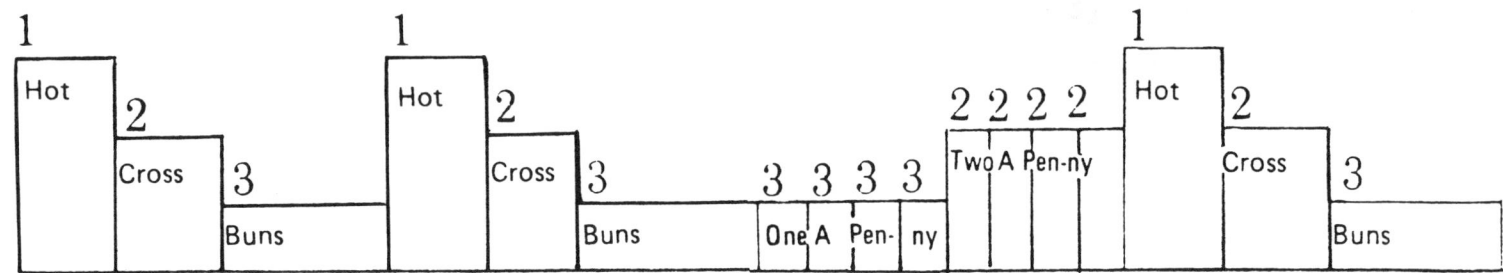

1215

The Piano Keyboard

Darken both the groups of 2 and 3 black keys (twins and triplets.)
Then, keep your eyes on the page and *feel* each group of black keys on your piano.
Do this until it is easy.

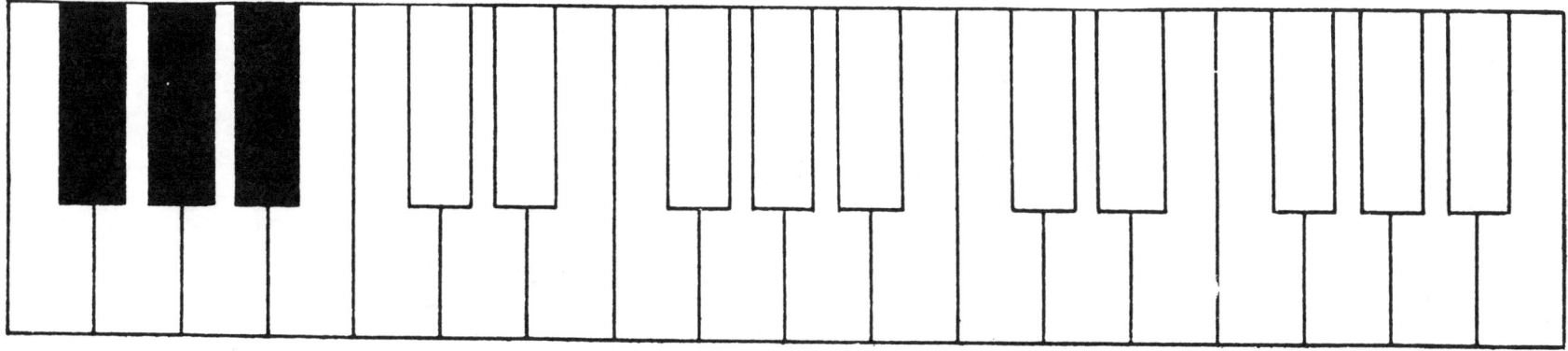

Again, darken all of the black keys.
Keep your eyes on the page as you find all of the twins and triplets on the piano keyboard.

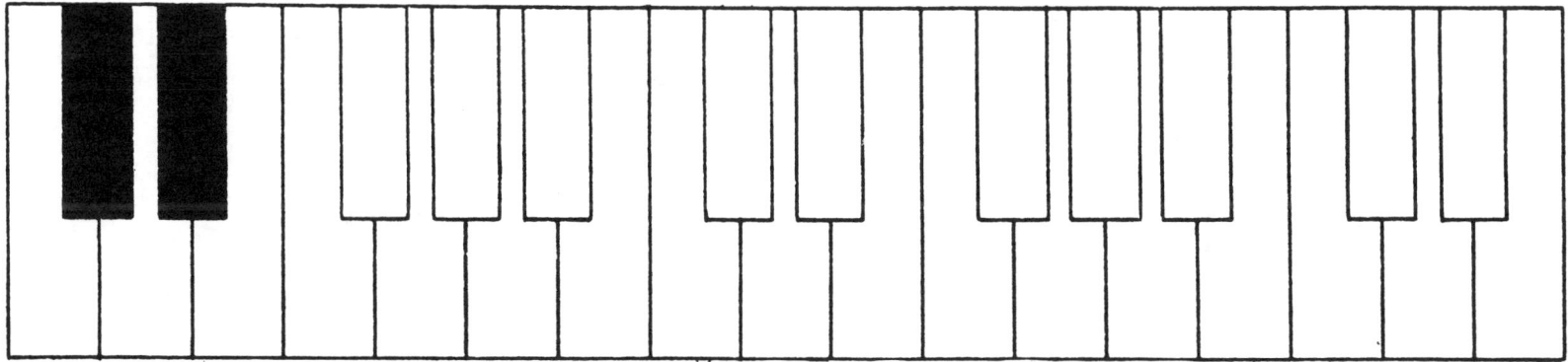

Finally, mix the two's and three's.
Be sure to find them without looking down.

Bugle Call

Play this high and low on your piano as you transpose to different keys.

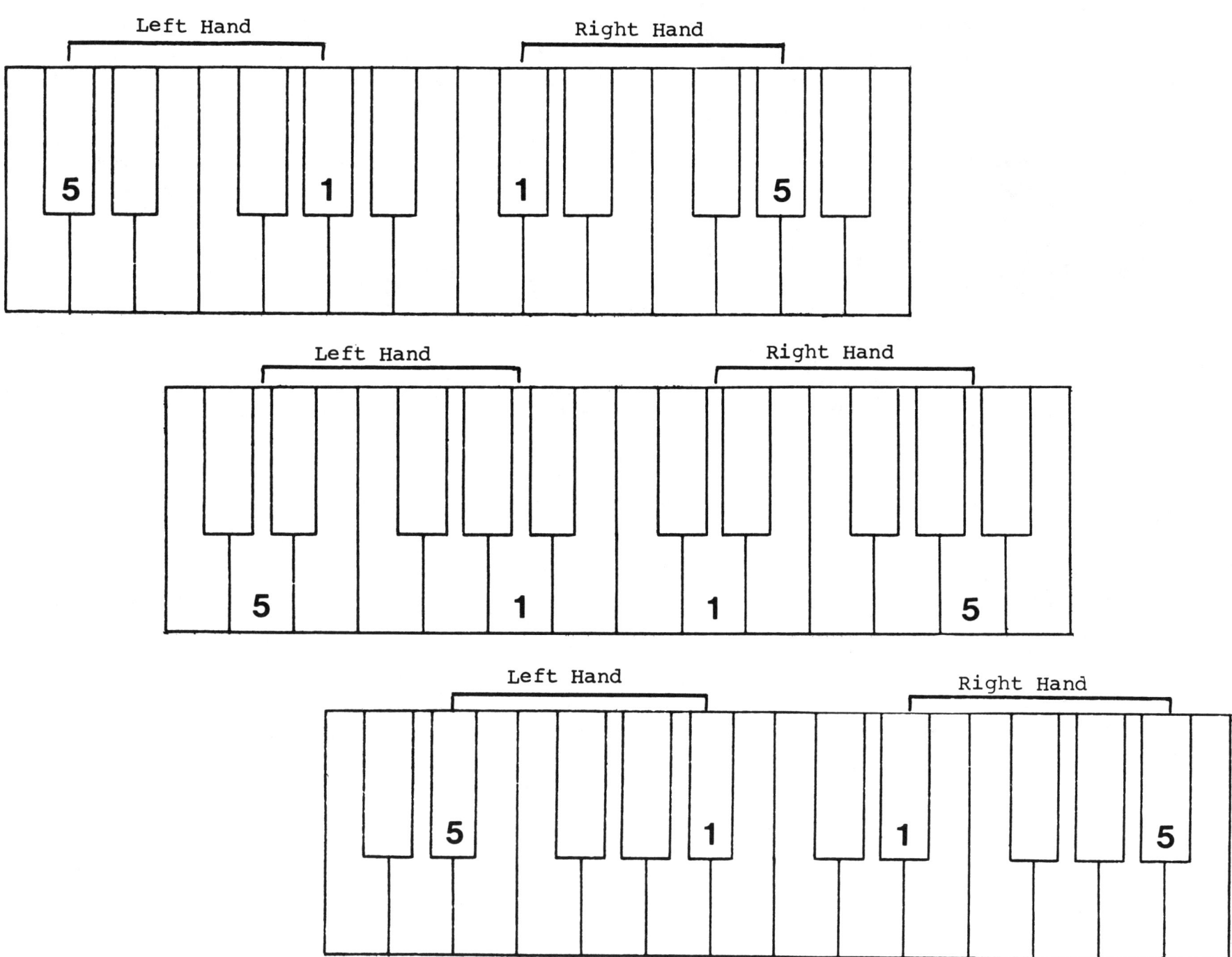

The Musical Alphabet

The piano keyboard uses the seven letters of the alphabet from A to G. Remember where the letters are in relation to the triplets and twins.

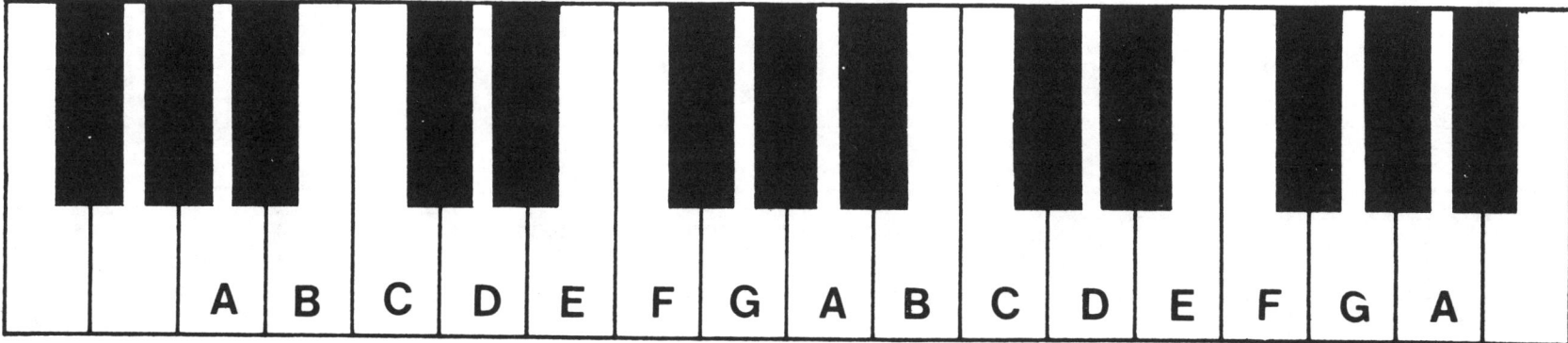

Fill in the A, B, C's on this keyboard.

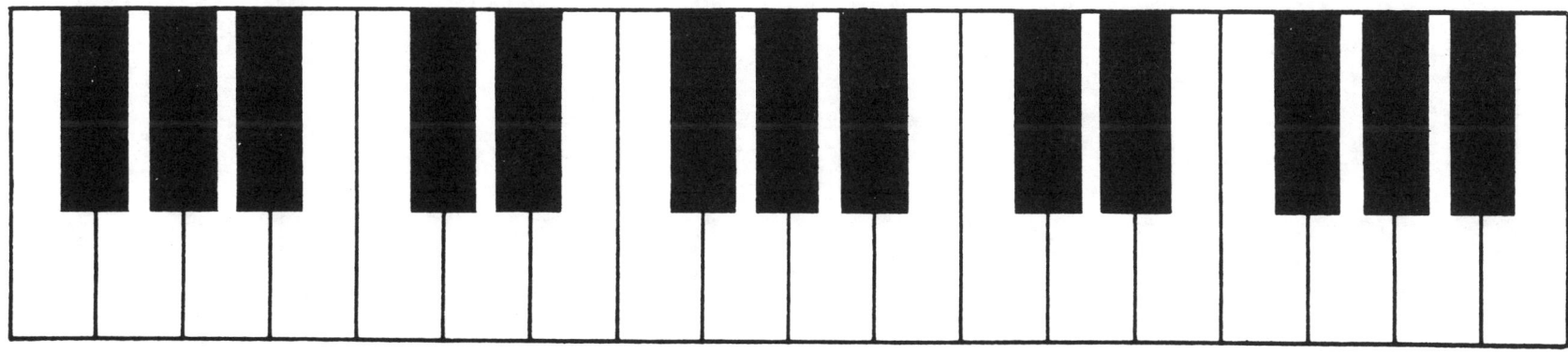

1215

Up and Down
(Fill-in)

Make a circle on the correct keys for playing "Up and Down". Refer to page 11 of *The Way to Play* if necessary. Then play each key to be sure you are correct.

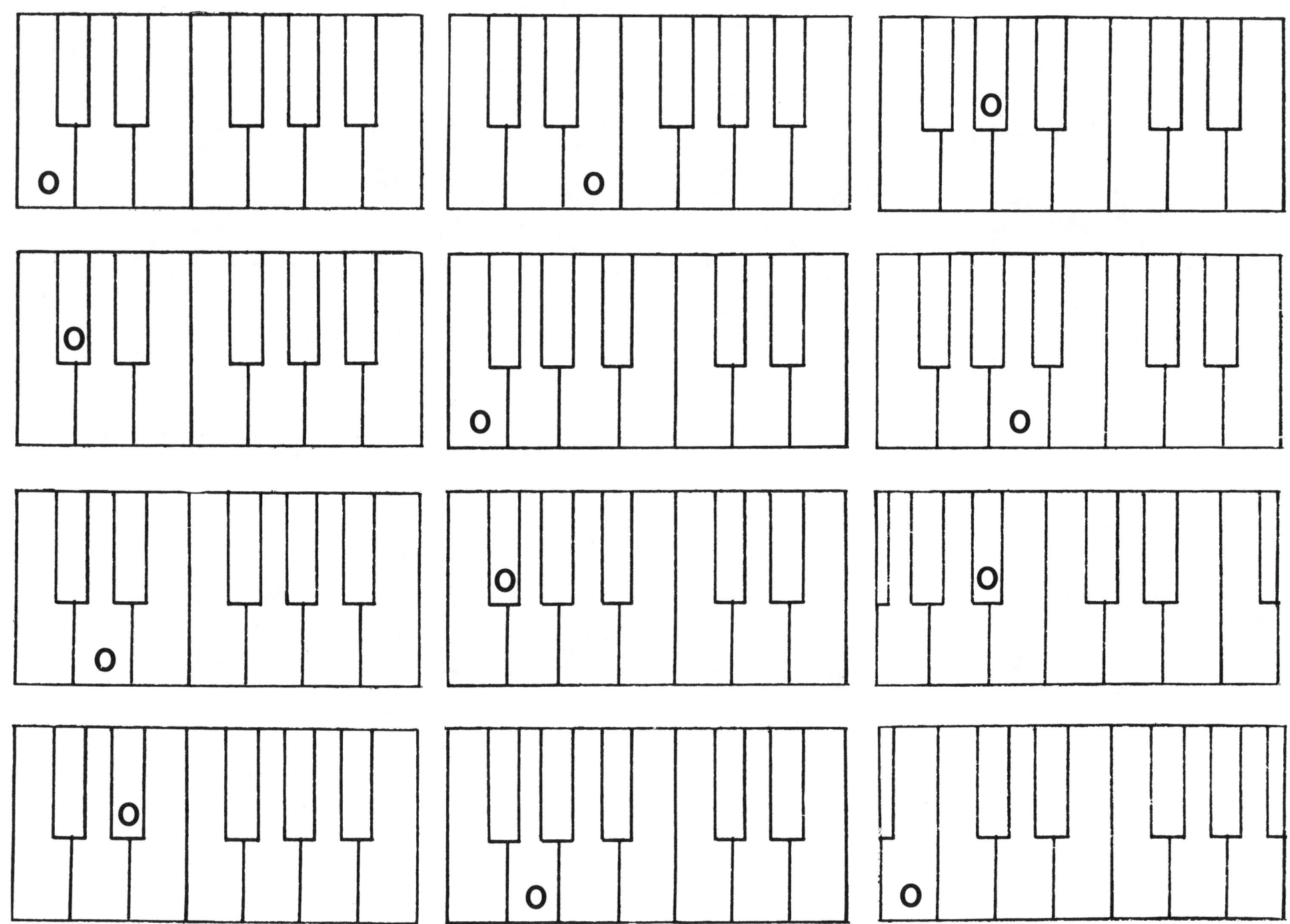

1215

Keyboard Fill-in

Write the letter name of every other white key beginning on A.

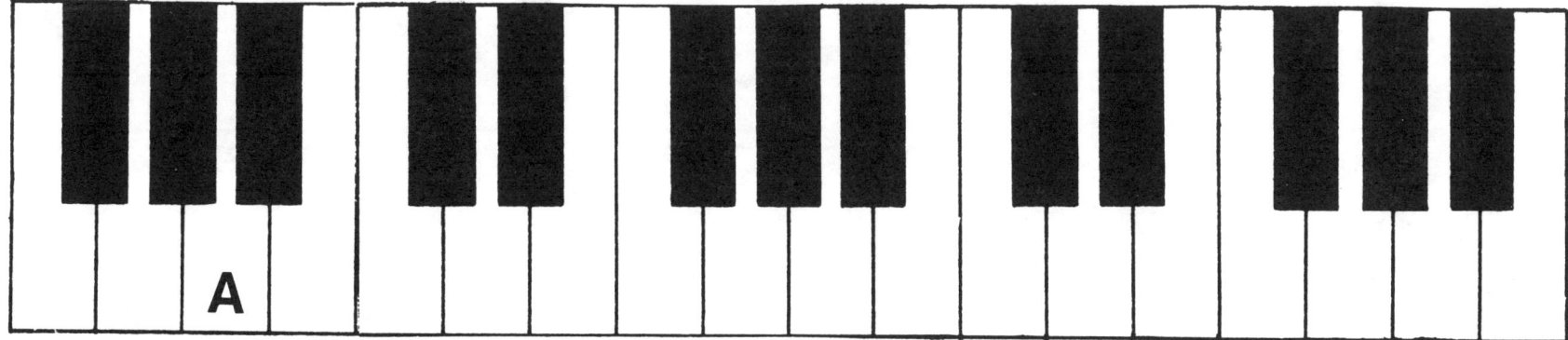

Write the letter name of every other white key beginning on C.

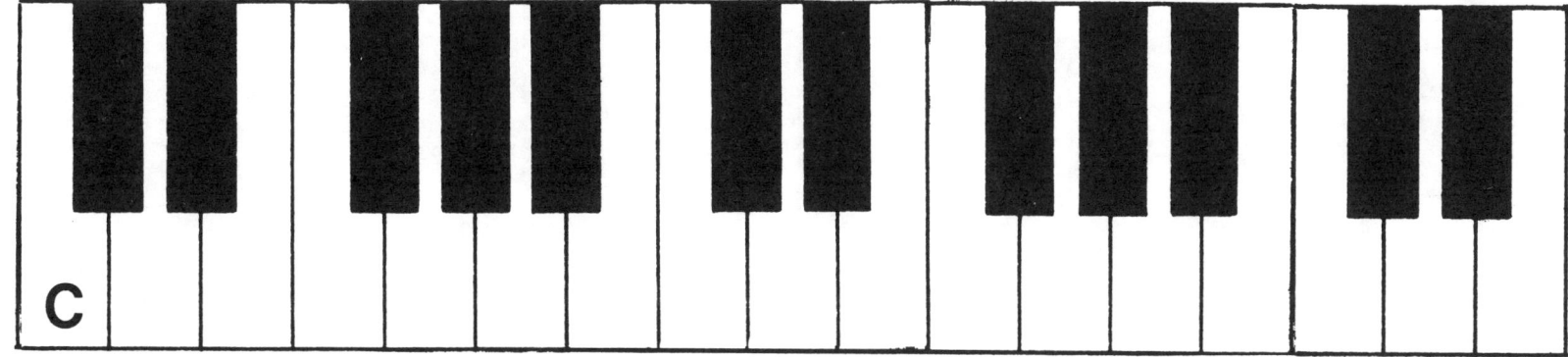

Write the letter name of every white key beginning on F.

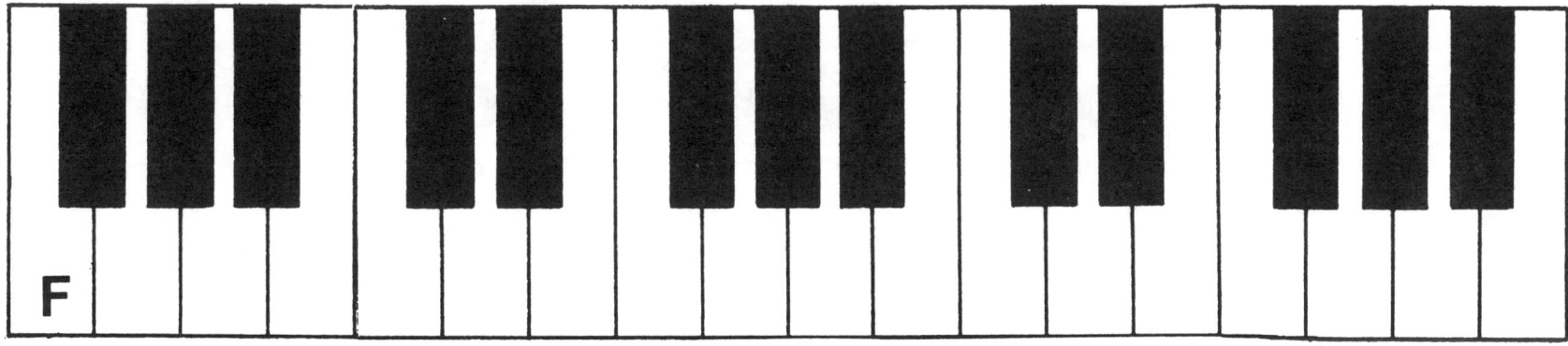

Melodies by Skips

This melody moves by skips. Notice its shape and that some notes are repeated.
Play first the right hand, then the left hand.

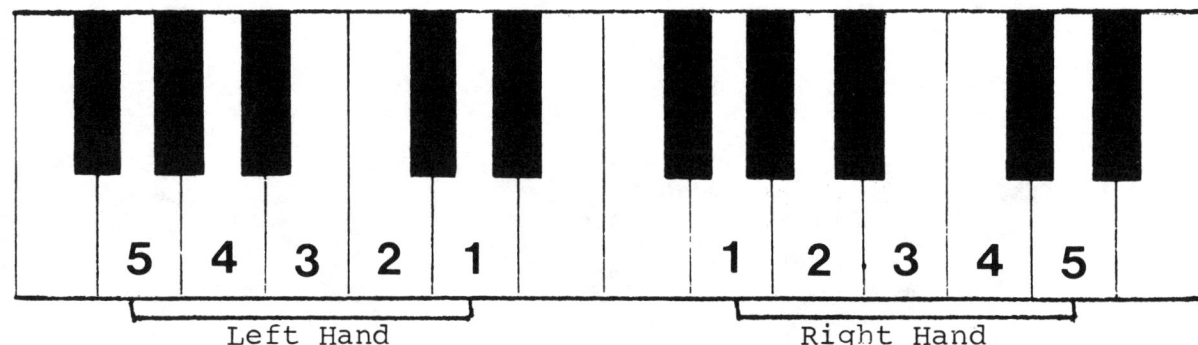

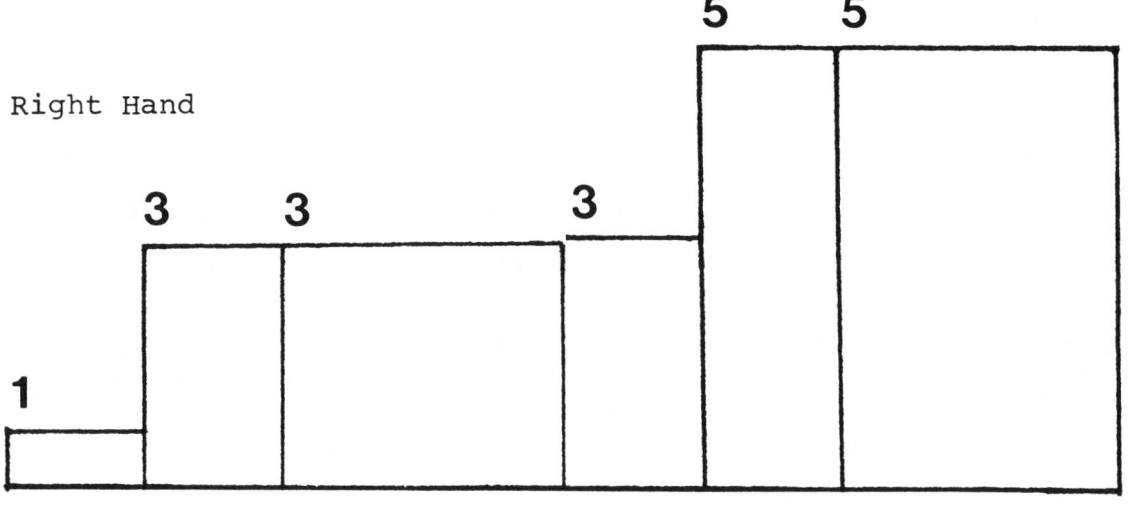

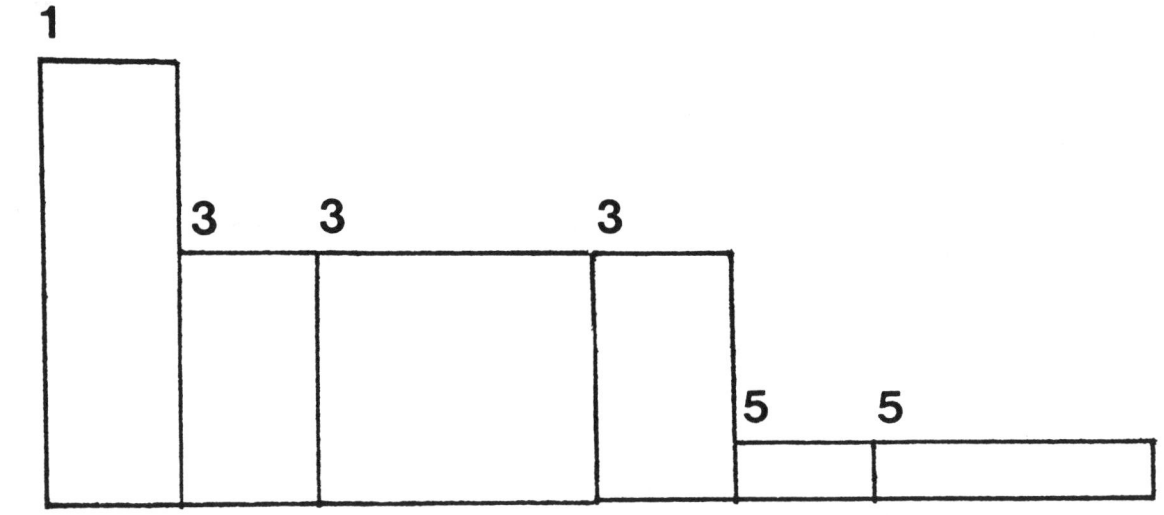

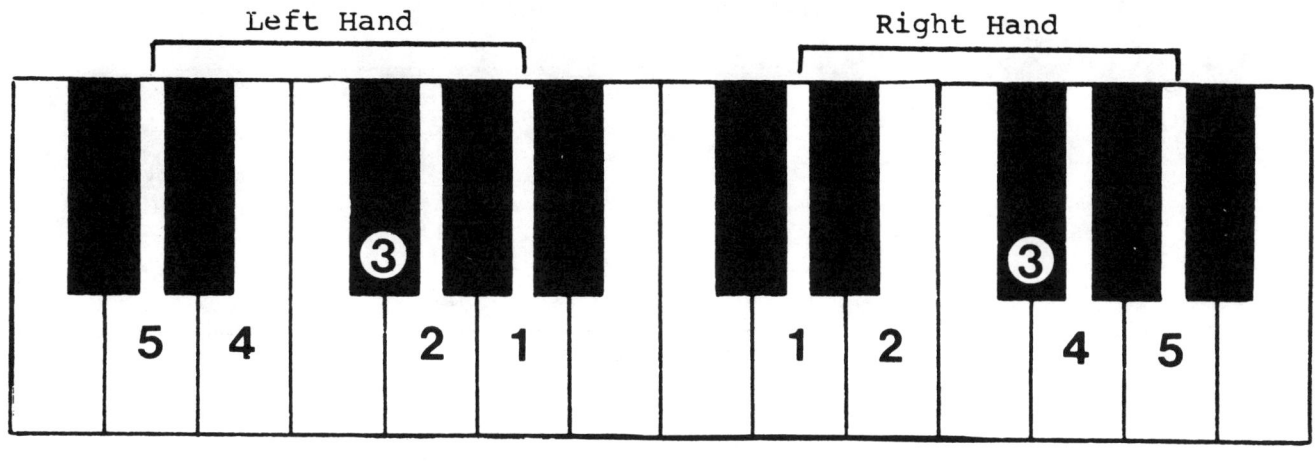

First, draw lines under each number to show the shape of the melody.
Then, find your place on the keyboard and play the melody.

Right Hand

```
                                              5
                    4                    4
        3                           3  3
              2                2
   1     1
```

Left Hand

```
   1     1
              2                2
        3                           3  3
                    4                    4
                                              5
```

1215

Melody Shapes

This melody moves by *steps*.
Notice its shape.
Play first the right hand,
then the left hand.

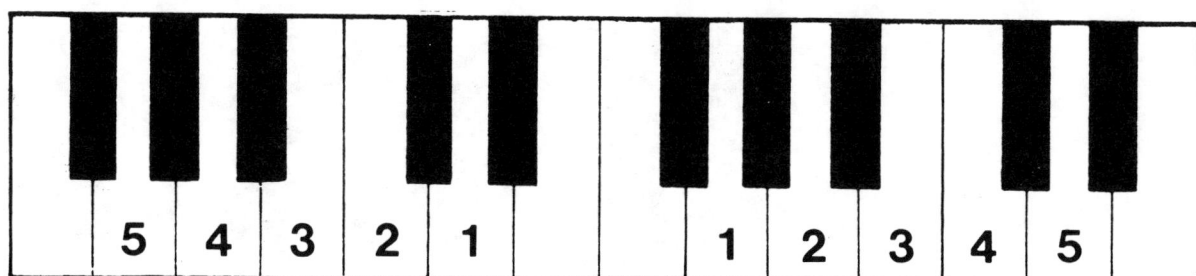

Right Hand

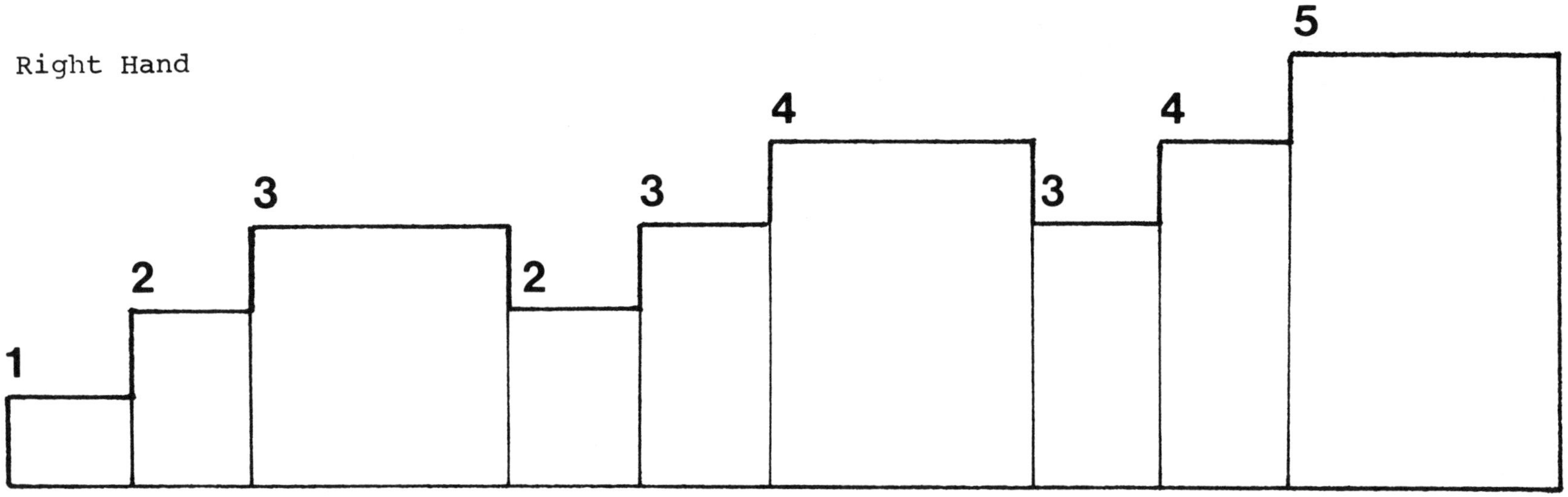

Left Hand

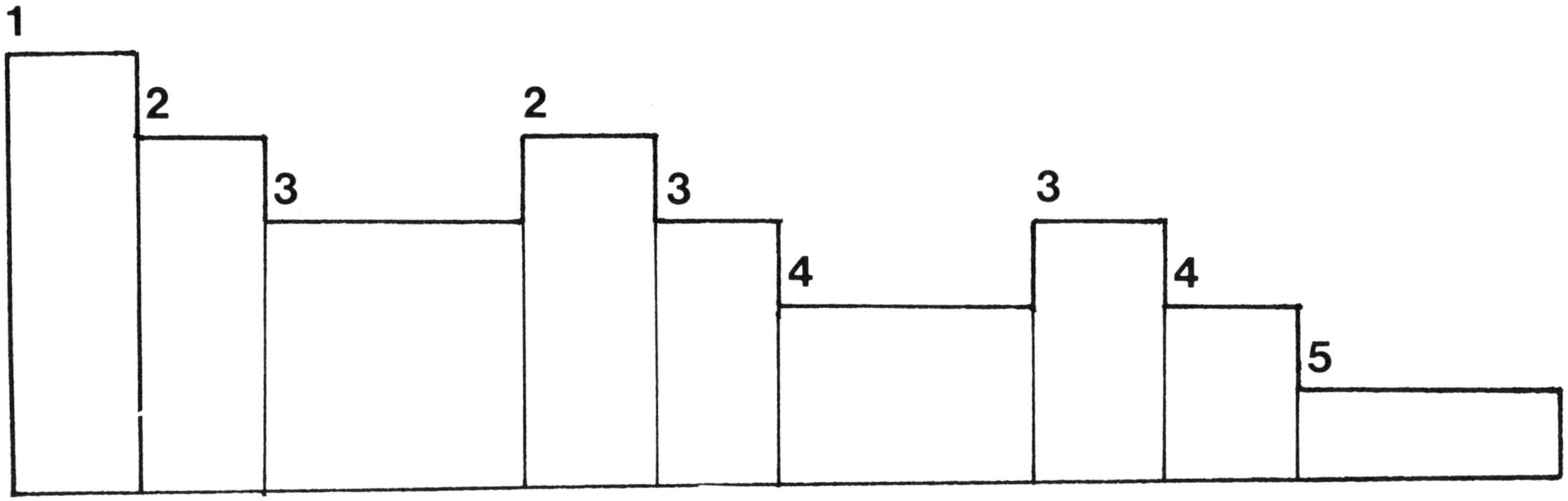

Melody Shapes

Draw lines over each word to show the shape of these melodies.
Then, play as indicated on the keyboard.

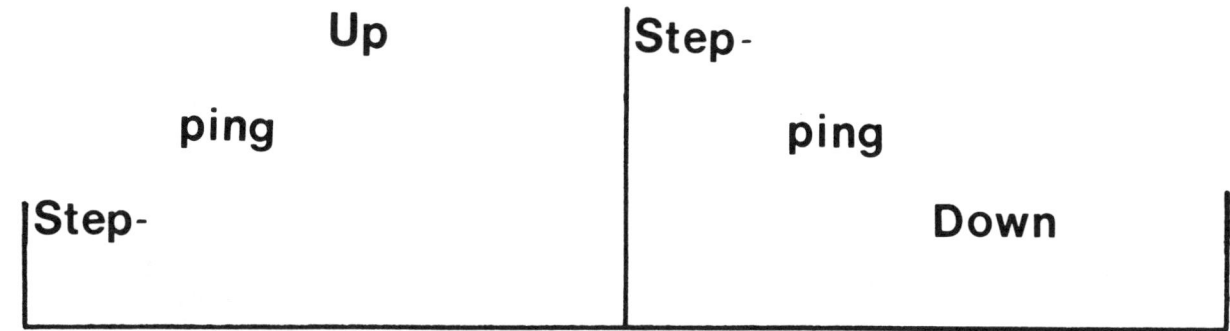

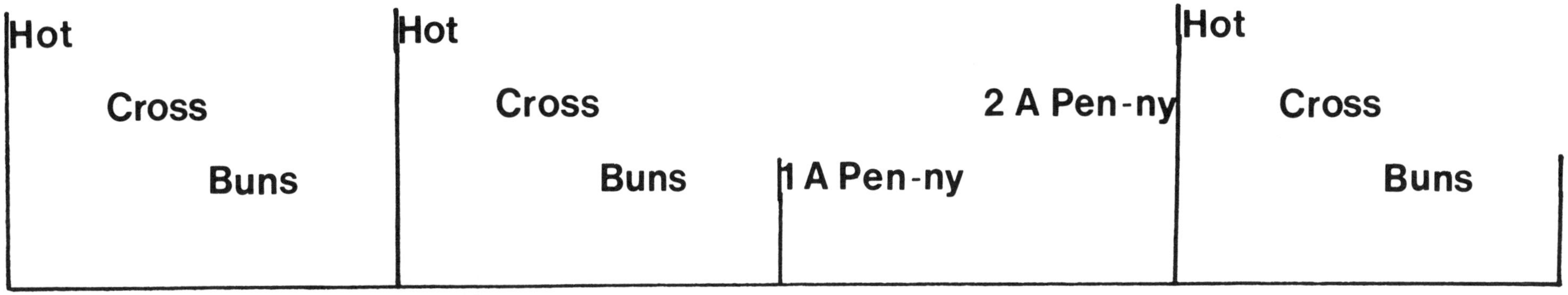

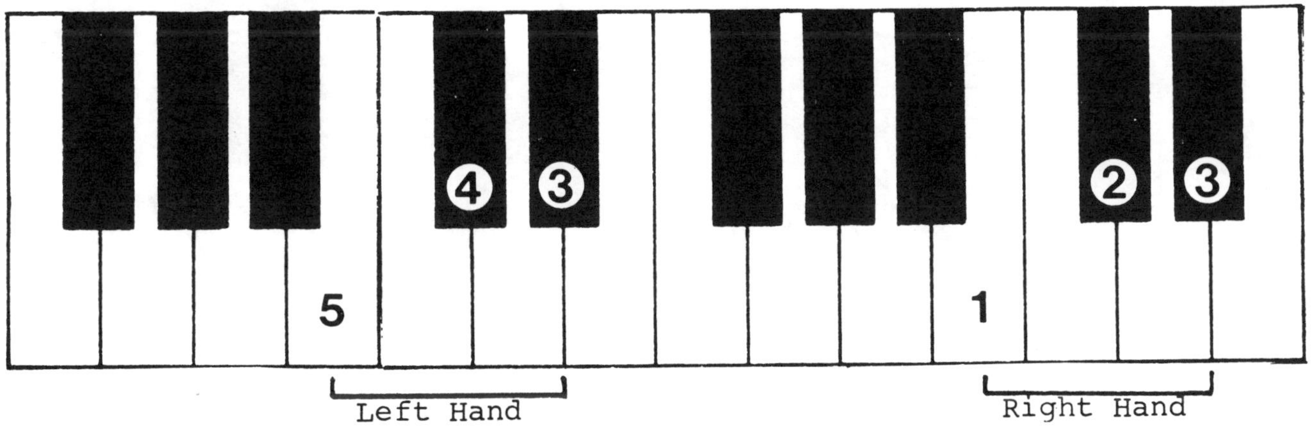

Steps and Skips

This melody moves by *steps and skips*.
Notice its shape.
Play first the right hand,
then the left hand.

Right Hand

Left Hand

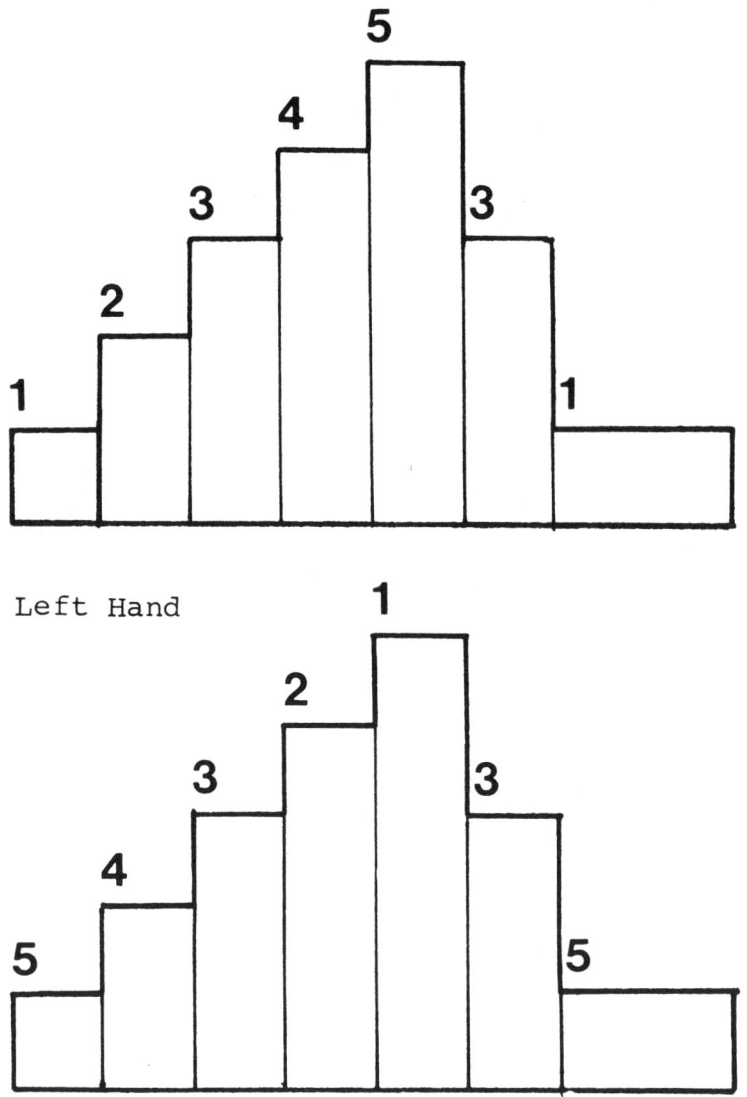
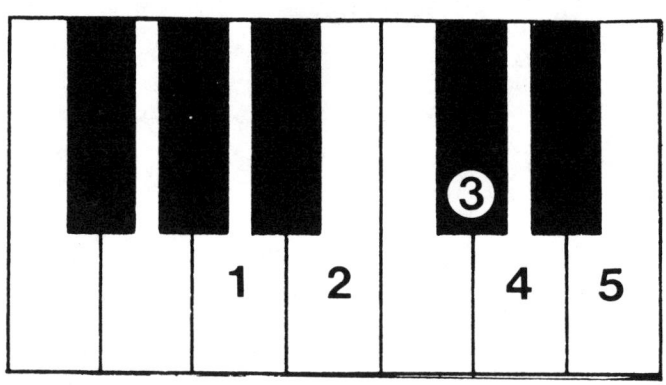
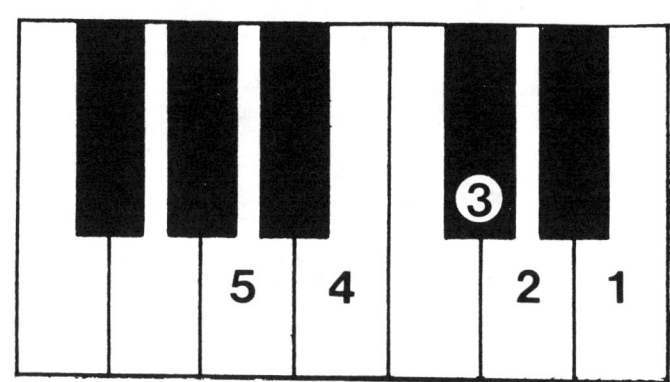

Keyboard Fill-in

First find all of the A's, then fill in the rest of the letters.

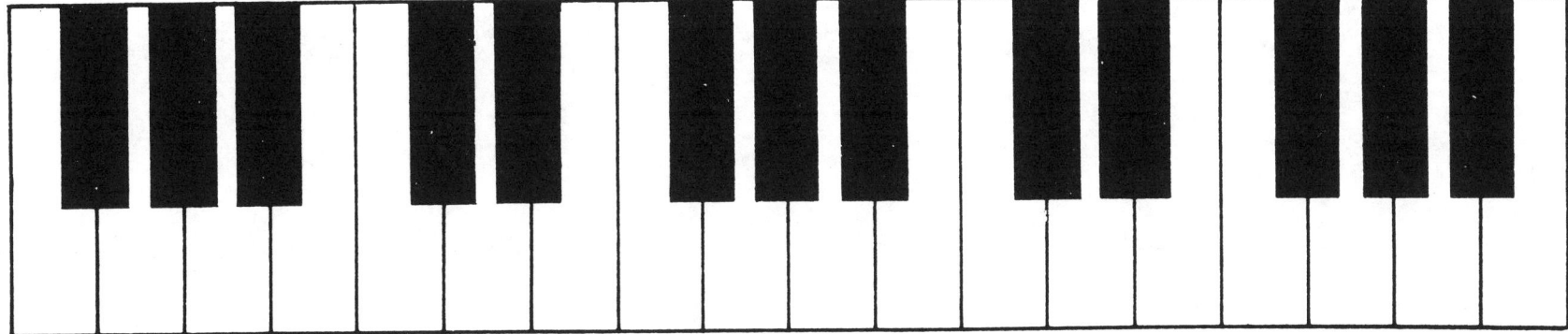

Write the letters from C to C.

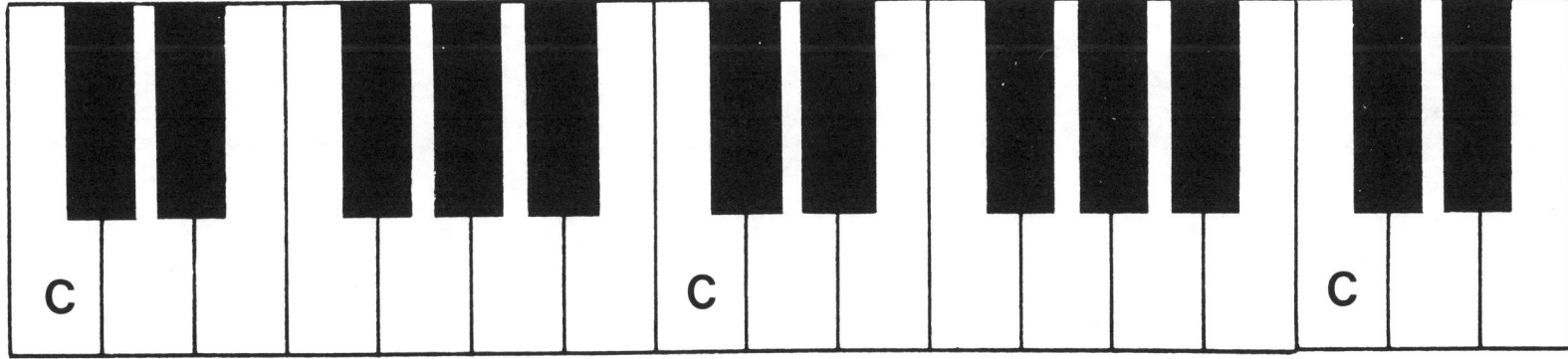

The Grand Staff

Find and play the A, B, C's of the Grand Staff.
Say the name of each as you play it and don't look at the keyboard.

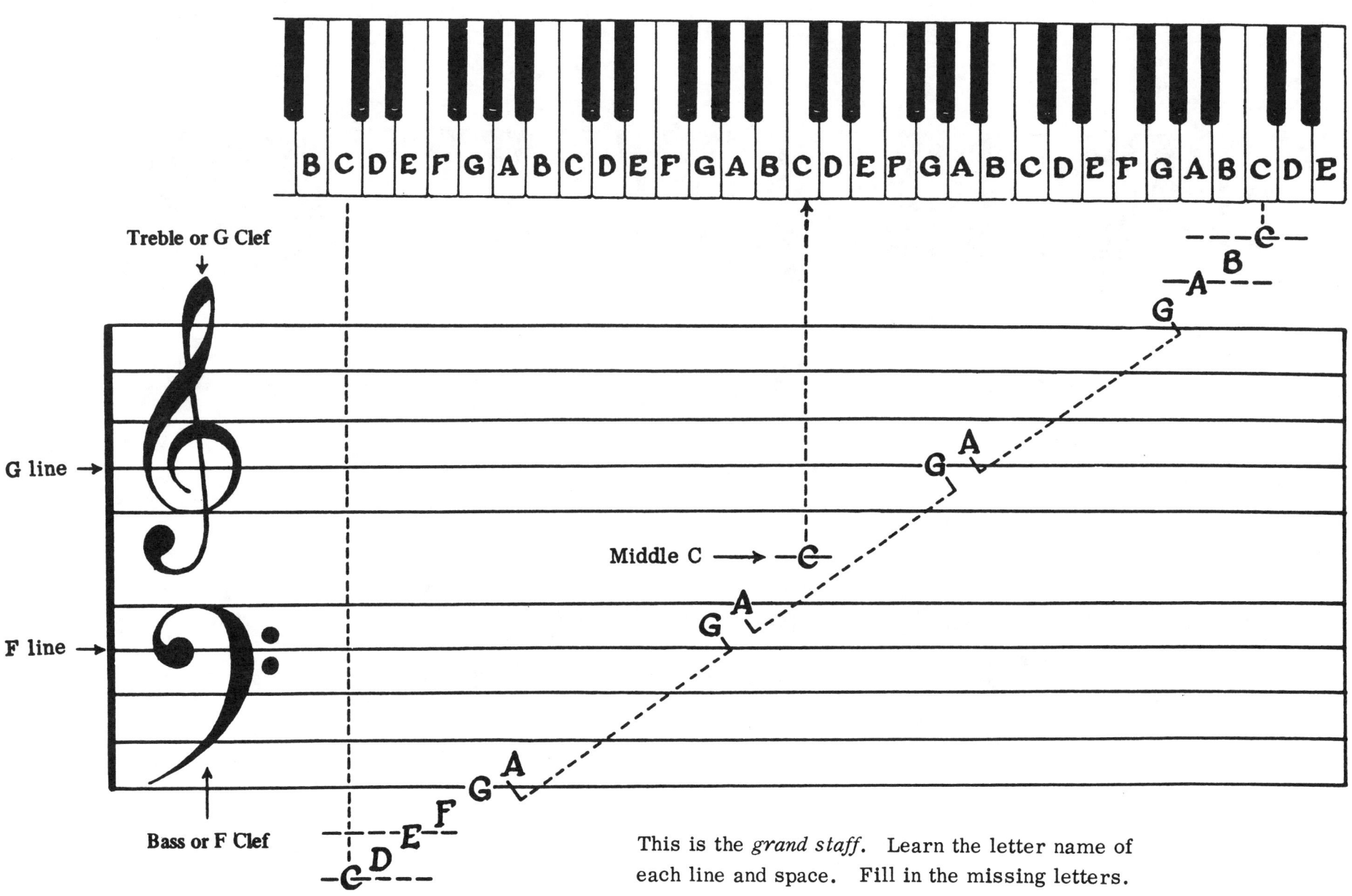

This is the *grand staff*. Learn the letter name of each line and space. Fill in the missing letters.

1215

Note Finding

Put the letter name on each key which has a dot.

Then, find and play that note on your piano without looking at your hands.

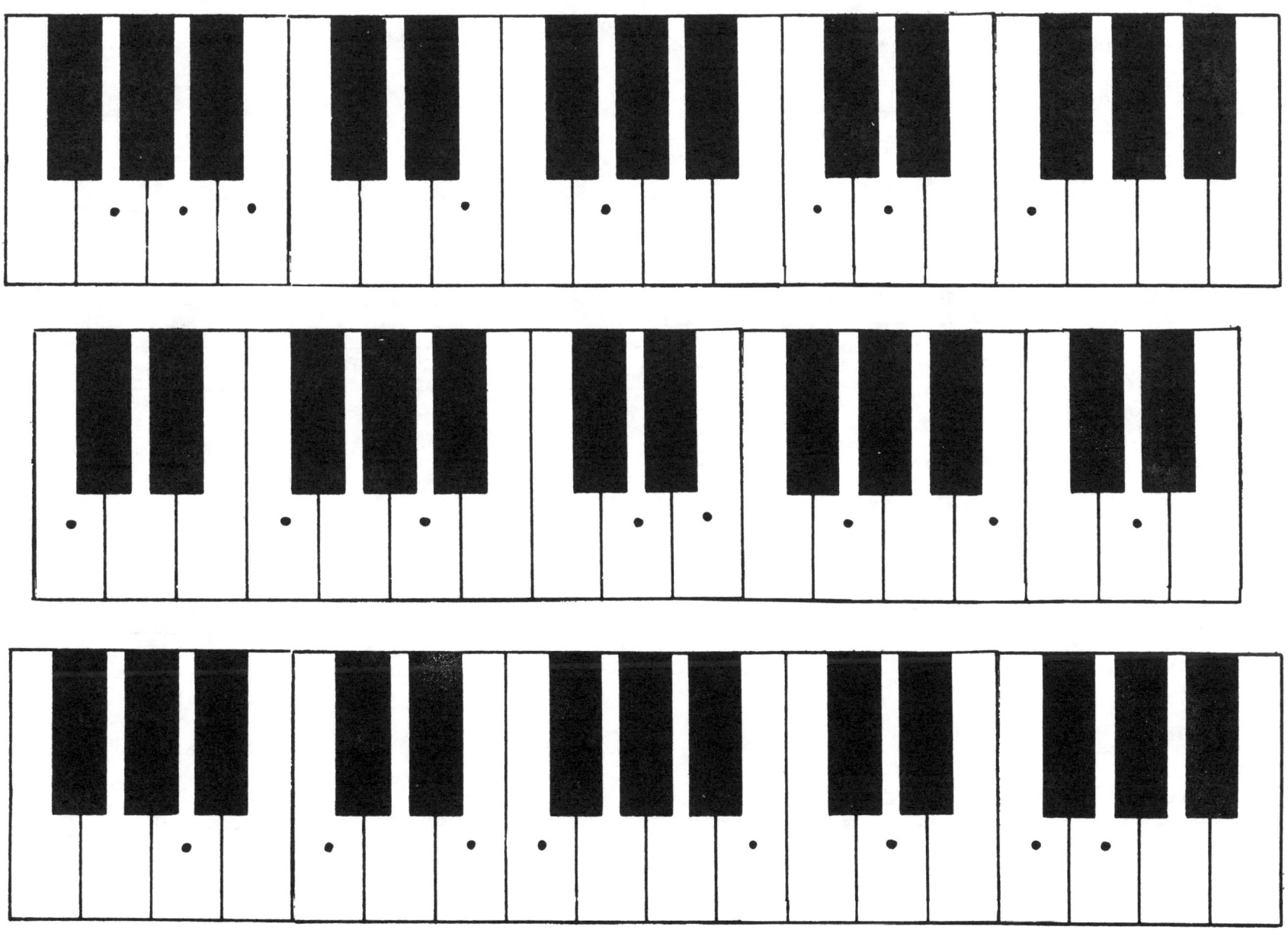

1215

Key Signatures

The key of C♯ Major has seven sharps.

Very little music is written in the keys of C♯ or C♭ so we will work on the other six keys.
Write the sharp key signatures in treble and bass clef.

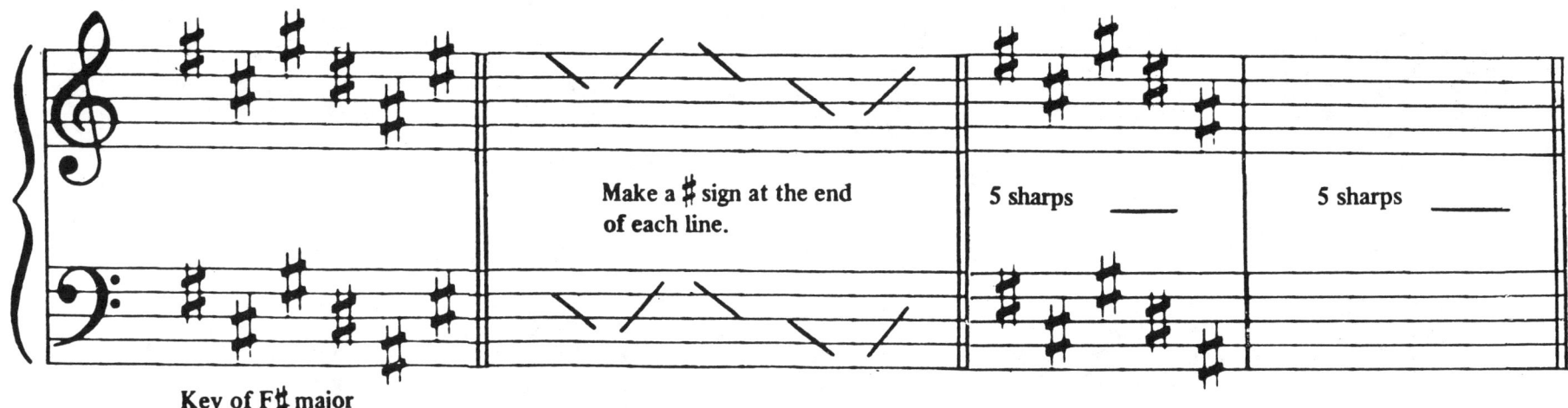

Key of F♯ major · Make a ♯ sign at the end of each line. · 5 sharps ___ · 5 sharps ___

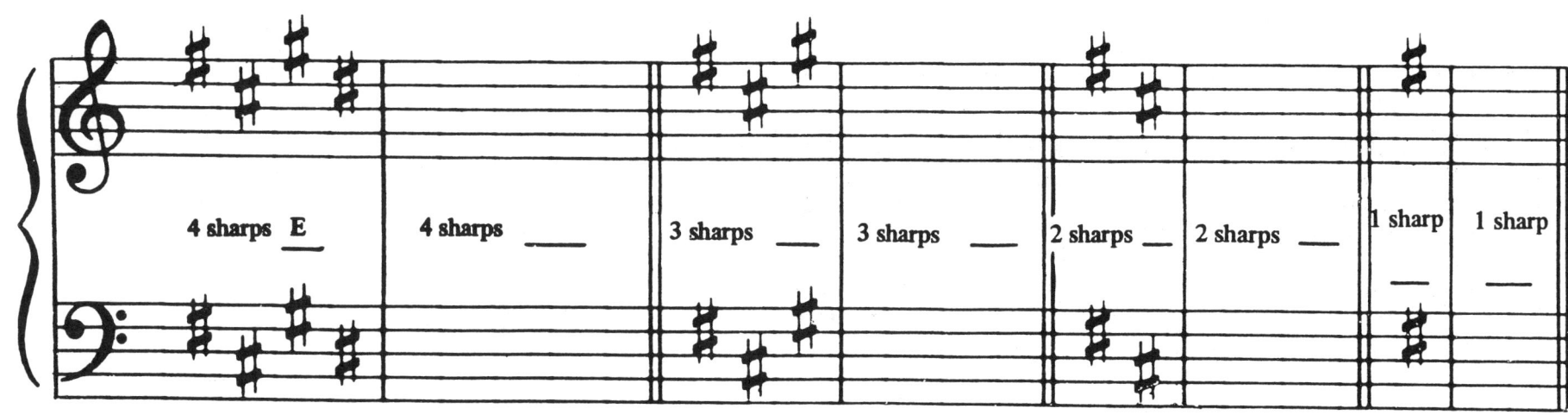

4 sharps E · 4 sharps ___ · 3 sharps ___ · 3 sharps ___ · 2 sharps ___ · 2 sharps ___ · 1 sharp · 1 sharp

Key Signatures

The key of C♭ Major has seven flats.

Write the flat key signatures in treble and bass clef.

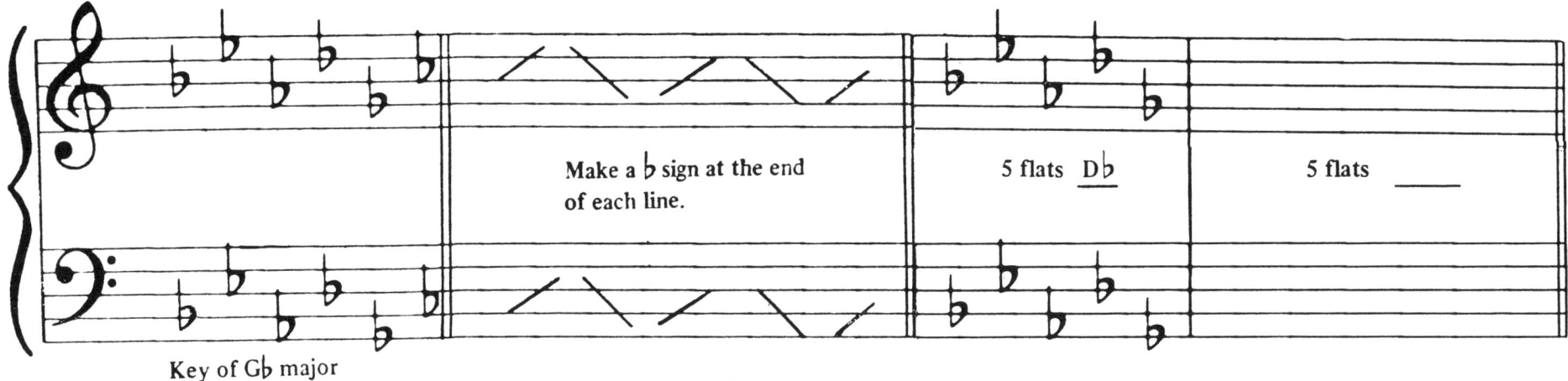

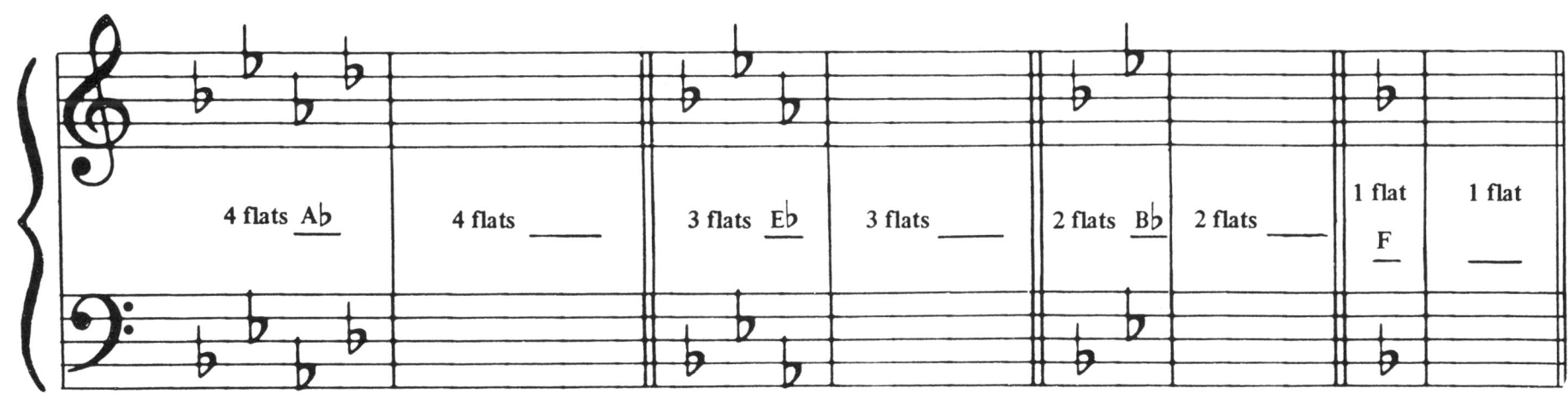

Play the sharp for each of these letters, then write it on the keyboard below.

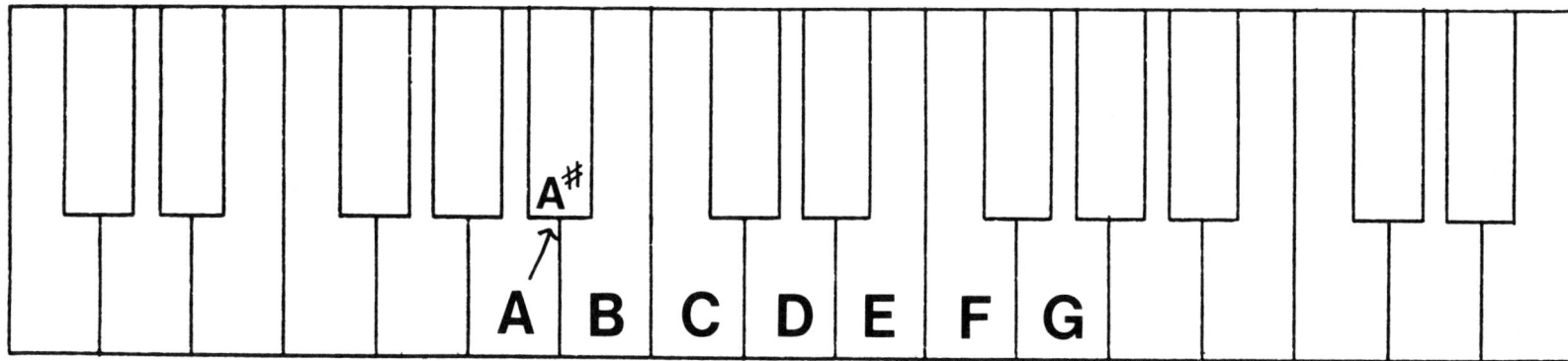

Play the flat for each of these letters, then write it on the keyboard.

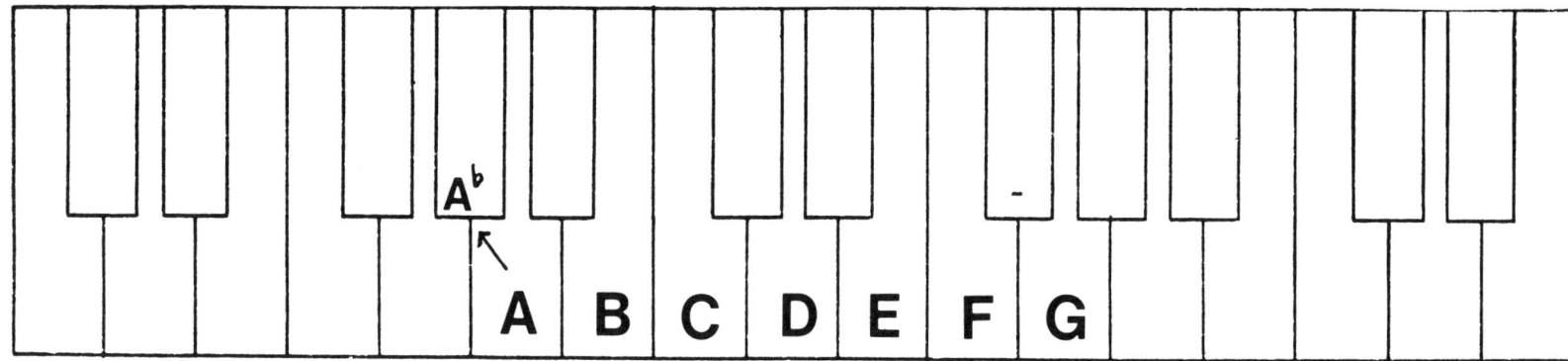

Key Signatures

Fill in these key signatures.

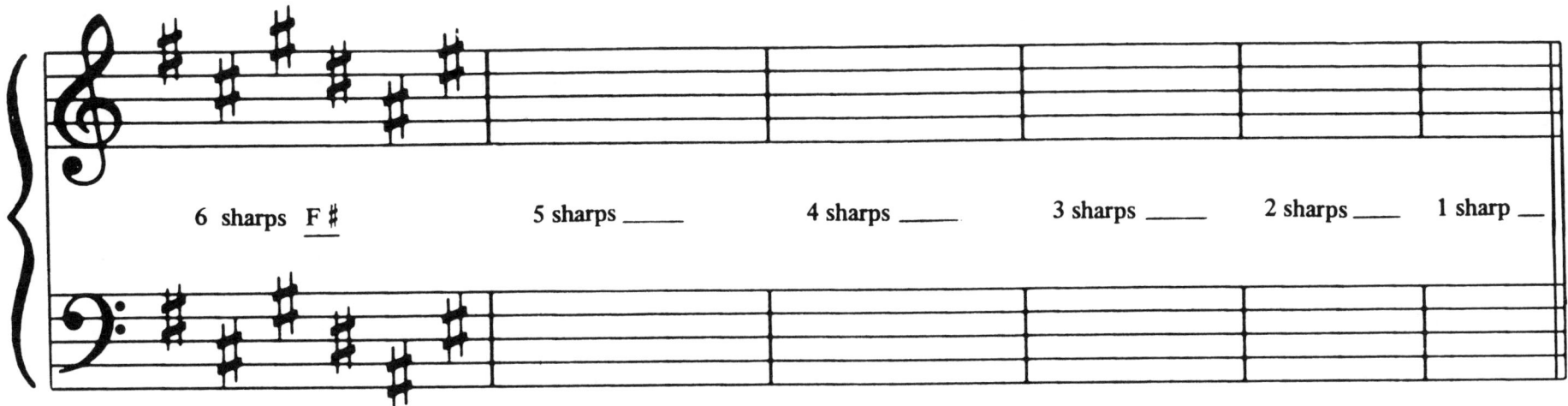

6 sharps F#   5 sharps ____   4 sharps ____   3 sharps ____   2 sharps ____   1 sharp ____

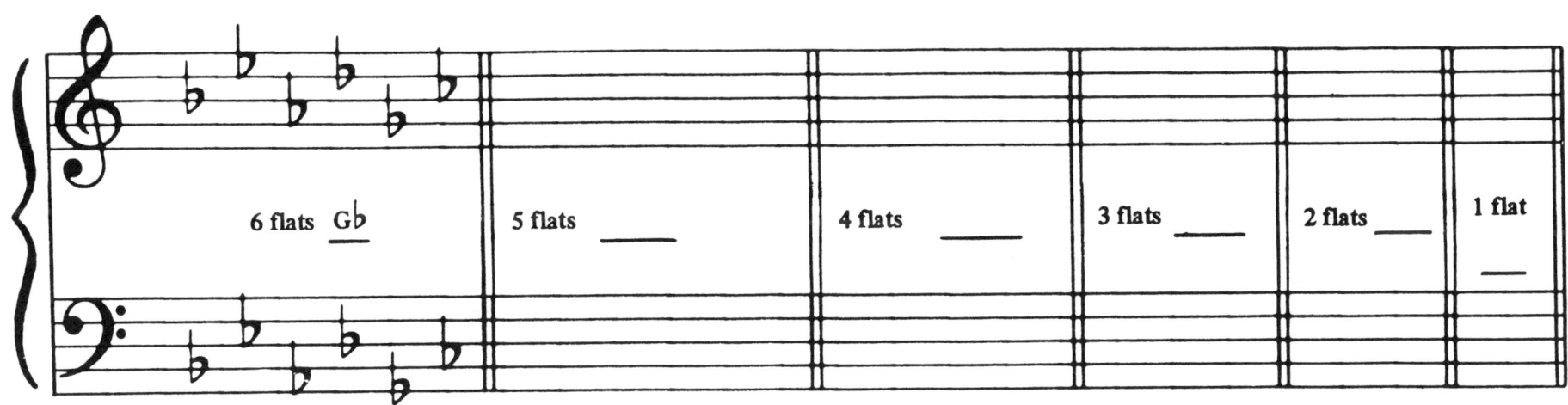

6 flats G♭   5 flats ____   4 flats ____   3 flats ____   2 flats ____   1 flat ____

Melodic Reading

1. First, notice the repeated notes and skips. Then, as you play this, count "Quarter, quarter, half note." Transpose to F and E major.

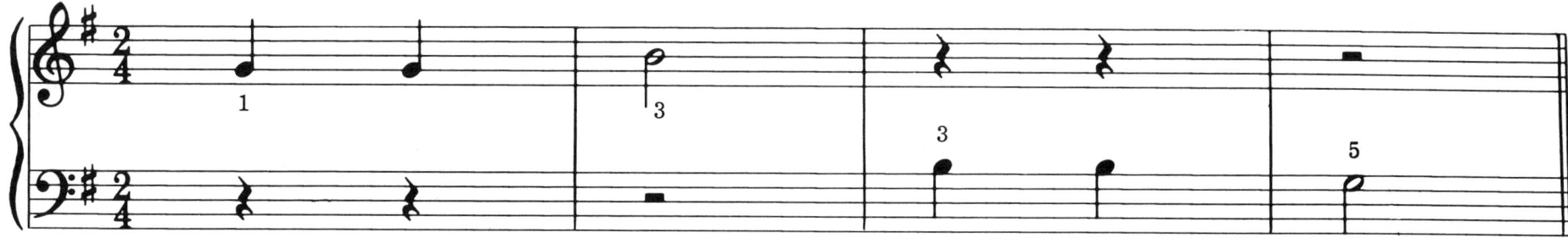

2. Notice the time signature and count this as you play. Transpose to E♭ and F major.

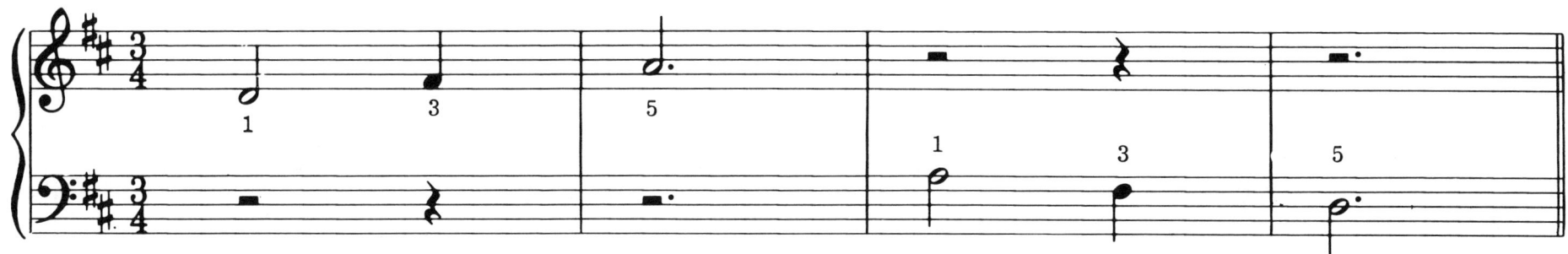

3. Look at this melody, then compare it with number 2. How are they different? Transpose to D♭ and E major.

Hot Cross Buns

1. Fill in the missing notes.

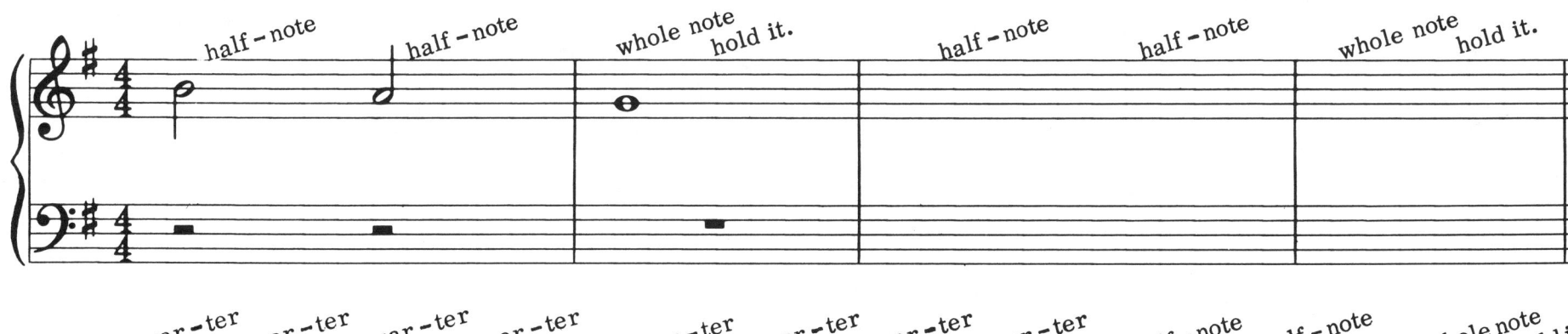

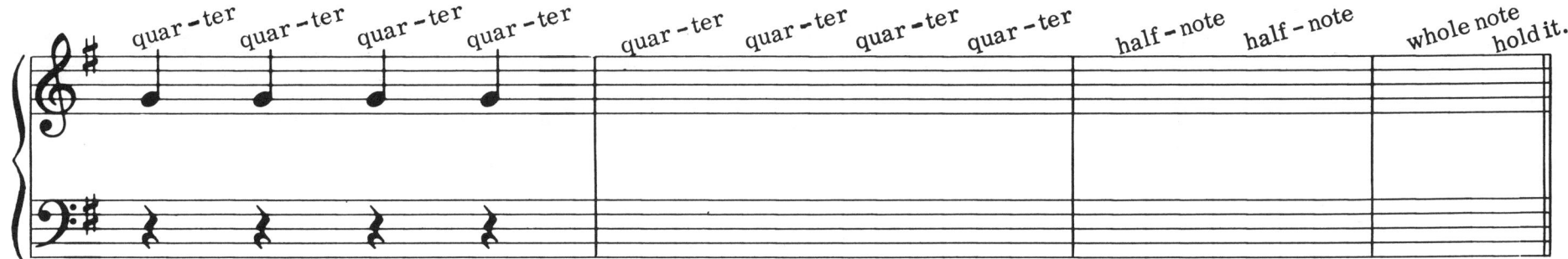

2. Write the letter names in both treble and bass clefs.

Grand Staff

Mary Had a Little Lamb

1. First, play as written in the key of E major. Then transpose to F, E♭ and D major.

Variation

2. Play this variation, then transpose to F♯, G and A♭ major.

Mary Had a Little Lamb

(Variations)

1. Improvise several variations, then write your favorite one here.

2. Try more variations in other keys and finally notate one here.

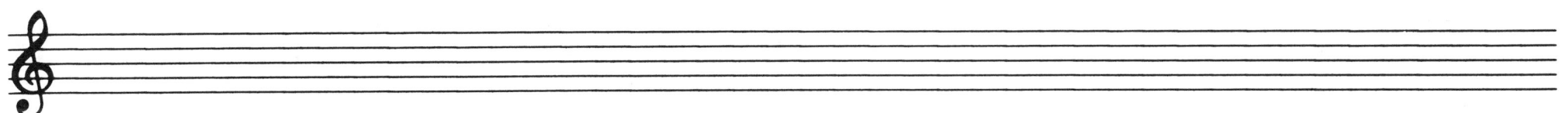

Melodic Variations

1. Sightread, then transpose to D, D♭, C and F major.

2. Now try this one as written, then transpose to E, F and G♭ major.

Melodic Changes

1. Make up many new melodies using these ideas. Then write one of them using the blank measures to notate your new melody.

2. Again improvise, then write your melody in the blank measures.

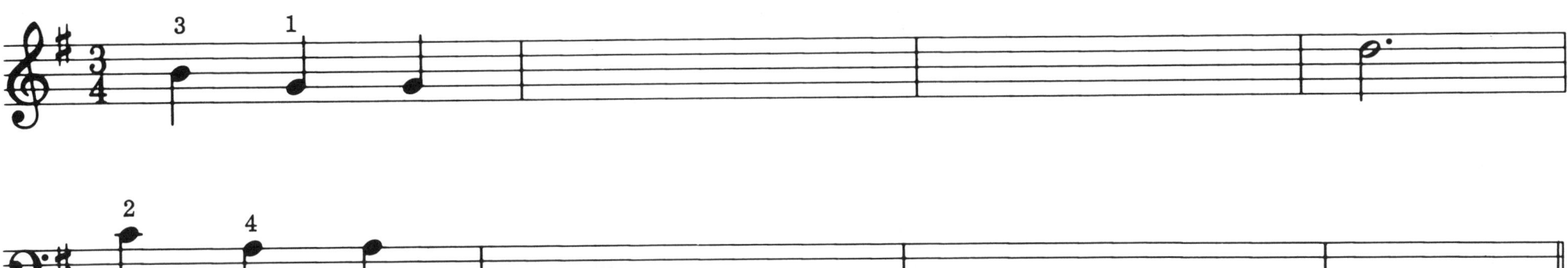

Old Woman

1. Play "Old Woman" as written, then transpose to G, A♭ and E major.

Swing Song

2. Sing the kind of note (quarter, half-note, etc.) as you play this in D♭, E♭ and F major.

Key Signature Review

1. Make flat key signatures in treble and bass clefs.

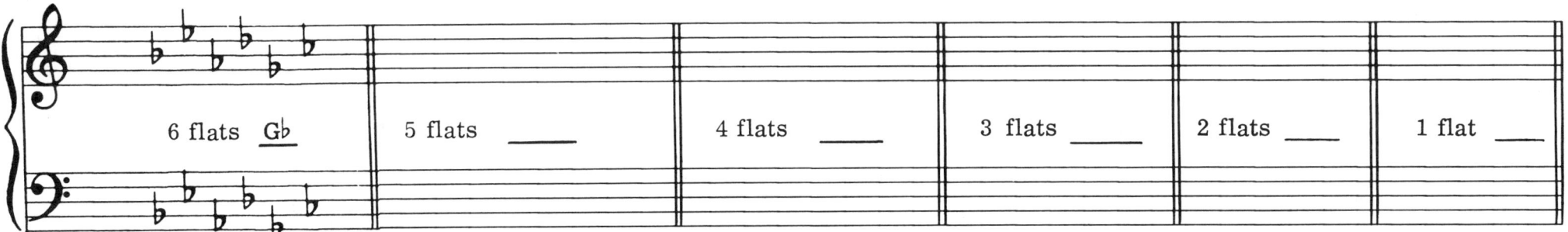

2. Make sharp key signatures in the treble and bass clefs.

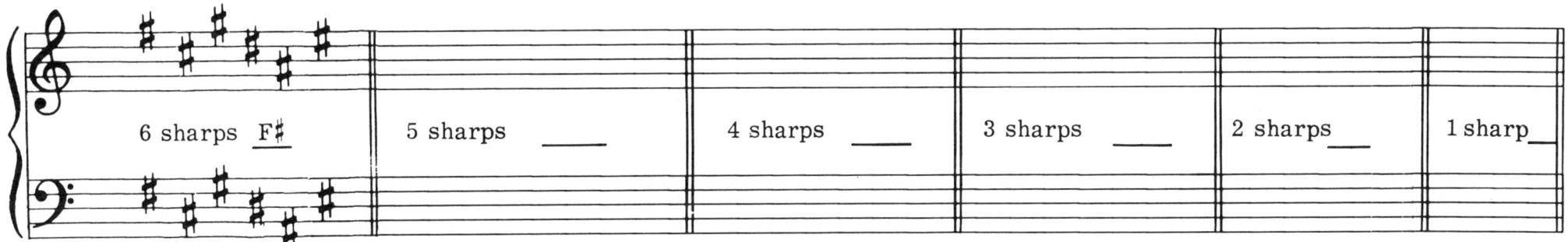

Listening Game

3. Listen carefully as you play this melody.   Then make others of your own.

Sweetly Sings the Donkey
(Variations)

1. Sightread this variation then transpose to D♭, C and B major.

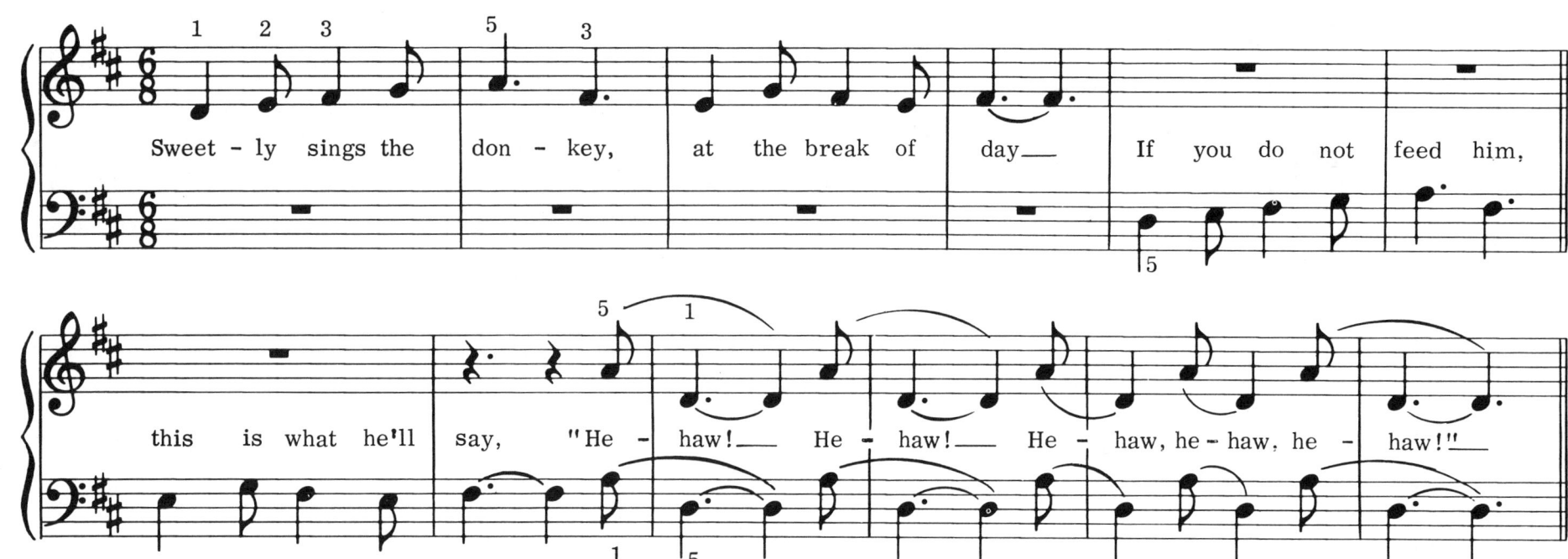

Skipping

2. Transpose to D♭, E, F and G major.

Question and Answer

1. Play both of these Questions and Answers several times. Then make up new Answers for the Questions. Finally, make up new Questions as well as Answers. Write your two favorite Questions and Answers below.